What
Mennonites
Believe

What Mennonites Believe

J.C. Wenger

Revised Edition

HERALD PRESS
Scottdale, Pennsylvania
Waterloo, Ontario

The paper used in this publication is recycled and meets the minimum requirements of American National Standard for Information Sciences—Permanence of Paper for Printed Library Materials, ANSI Z39.48-1984.

Photo Credits: page 9, Jean-Claude Lejeune; page 23, Cheryl Morgan; page 31, MCC photo by Harvey Harman; page 75, Jim Whitmer.

WHAT MENNONITES BELIEVE
Copyright © 1977, 1991 by Mennonite Board of Missions, Elkhart, IN 46514. Published 1977. Revised edition 1991.
    Published by Herald Press, Scottdale, Pa. 15683.
    Released simultaneously in Canada by Herald Press, Waterloo, Ont. N2L 6H7. All rights reserved.
Library of Congress Catalog Number: 90-084719
International Standard Book Number: 0-8361-3542-3
Printed in the United States of America
Inside design by Paula M. Johnson

4 5 6 7 8 9 10 98 97 96 95

Distributed overseas by Mennonite Board of Missions, Inc., 1251 Virginia Avenue, Harrisonburg, VA 22801.

Contents

Foreword

We live in a world which often seems to have lost its way. The communities which held us together are coming unglued. Drugs and violence and injustice stalk our cities. Rich people need binoculars to see the poor people on the other side of the gap.

Followers of Jesus can find new meaning, joy, and direction, even in today's world. Among the many who follow Christ are Mennonites, who take their name from Menno Simons, a Frisian (Dutch) Reformer of the sixteenth century.

This book explores beliefs held in common by Christians of all denominations and highlights those stressed by Mennonites. As they experience the modern pressures all Christians face, not all Mennonites emphasize the same beliefs.

However, Mennonites generally see God's

forgiveness of sins and our choice to live rightly, even in the face of suffering, as inseparable.

Mennonites believe a key way to live rightly is to reject war and violence and model the way of peace.

Mennonites believe that the courageous living Jesus asks of his followers requires Christians to band together in community. This is how they receive the strength they need to model for the world a different way of life. A troubled planet needs such emphases.

Until the nineteenth century, most Mennonites were found in Europe and North America. During the twentieth century, however, missions, relief and service activities, and the grace of God have resulted in a worldwide Mennonite fellowship.

—*Michael A. King*

ONE

How Mennonites and Other Christians Are Alike

Every church denomination has its reason for being different from other groups of believers.

Sometimes the reason is simply geographic—the group came into being in a certain area.

Sometimes the reason is historical—the group began in a certain area under special circumstances. The group may follow a certain powerful leader. Some groups, unfortunately, develop

9

when schism or disagreements within a group cause division.

Therefore, sometimes Christian groups forget how much biblical truth they hold in common with Christians everywhere. This is perhaps especially true of smaller denominations—often referred to as sects.

This term was the idea of Ernst Troeltsch (1865-1923). He seemed to think that only the large state churches deserved the name *church*. The smaller free churches should then be seen as *sects*. (See explanation below of *state* and *free*.)

One reason for this may have been that the smaller groups sometimes held to an unusual belief or practice. At least this seems to be the way many people hear the word *sect* today. Indeed, *sect* actually suggests to many people that a group is unsound in faith.

FOLLOWERS OF CHRIST

Mennonites are sometimes seen as a sect, but Mennonites like to think of themselves simply as followers of Jesus Christ. They try to live out the New Testament teachings of Jesus.

Because of this emphasis on Christ and the Bible, Mennonites have many things in common with other Christian groups. The most important of these is that we serve the same Lord and obey his teachings.

A FREE CHURCH

One point of disagreement with some Christian groups is that the church should be a free church, not a state church. The free churches are those not established by law as the official religious bodies of the country or nation in which they are found.

Members of these free churches deeply want to be faithful Christians. They seek to be sound in faith and true to their Lord and Savior, Jesus Christ.

These free churches hold a vast body of Christian truth in common with the Catholic and Orthodox churches of history. Baptists and Methodists—to name two—share with Mennonites the free-church tradition. (In much of the modern world, of course, all denominations are now "free," not established by the government.) There are many convictions Christians hold in common.

A PERSONAL GOD

Christians believe in a great, personal God whose goodness, love, mercy, and power are unlimited. They believe God is finally in control of the world, although God gives up that control when exercising it conflicts with our free will.

God loves us as a parent loves a child. As a child's misbehavior can anger or sadden a parent, so does our sin anger and sadden God. This God has in mercy and grace created all things,

11

seen and unseen. Because God is a person, God knows, loves and guides us as children. God also has a plan for the world.

HUMAN BEINGS IN THE DIVINE IMAGE

This loving God wanted to have creatures to talk with, to be friends with. God was not content with the plants or even the rich world of animal life. Therefore, God made human beings in the image of God, male and female.

God created us with a moral nature, able to choose right and reject wrong. God gave us a capacity for unselfish and gracious love. We are capable of enjoying friendship with our Creator-God.

We are destined to live forever, either in bliss with God or in eternal separation from God. God put a monitor at the very center of our being. We call it our *conscience*. This helps us to know and do what is right.

God also gave us an inner awareness that we are responsible to God for our thoughts, words, and deeds. We call this sense of responsibility and accountability *free will*.

THE FALL INTO SIN

The story of the creation is beautifully described in Genesis, chapters 1 and 2. In chapter 3 we learn the dreadful story of our fall into sin. We did not remain in the good state in which we were created. In our freedom as persons, we chose to revolt against the Creator.

Worst of all, by the disobedience of Adam and Eve, we all became sinners. We call the results of this fall *original sin.* This means that as soon as we enter the world sin begins to affect us.

DIVINE REDEMPTION

The eternal love of God for fallen people was so great that God planned to rescue or save them. This salvation was provided when Jesus came into the world as a human and died for all our sins. The theme of salvation runs through the Old and New Testaments. God would one day send a redeemer into the world as a human, yet also as God in the flesh.

This promised one, Jesus, would teach his disciples about God and God's plan to save us from the tragic results of the fall. Later Jesus would die as a sacrifice for the sins of the whole world. Jesus would defeat the forces of sin and death through victorious resurrection from the dead.

When Jesus had ascended to heaven, God would send the promised Holy Spirit upon the people waiting for that new fullness. This God did on Pentecost. All this and much more was pointed to in the Old Testament. In the New Testament, the four Gospels and Acts describe its fulfillment.

DIVINE REVELATION

The Old Testament prophets interpreted and applied the great principles of the law of Moses (contained in the first five books of the Old Testament).

The prophets taught repentance and faith. They urged turning away from wrong ways. They gave personal and national guidance to Israel, the people of God. They kept alive the messianic hope—the hope that God would one day send a Savior.

The revelation of God began in the Old Testament and deepened with the coming of Jesus. The central message of the apostles of Jesus was that Jesus of Nazareth (who was crucified and resurrected about AD 30) was the Messiah or Christ. *Christ* is the Greek way of saying what is said by the Hebrew word for the *Anointed one*.

The revelation of God through Jesus Christ given in the New Testament is final and complete. This means that God the Creator is also a God of revelation and redemption—through Jesus Christ our Lord.

THE HOLY SPIRIT

The redemption of God through Jesus Christ comes to individual men and women through the good work of God's Holy Spirit. As we read the Word of God or hear it preached, this Spirit helps us know we are sinners.

The Spirit gently invites us to turn our lives

over to Christ. The Spirit changes the self of any who choose to turn away from sin. We call this change the *new birth*.

The Holy Spirit leads the new believer to higher ground spiritually and nudges her or him to respond to new understandings of God's will. In short, God through the Spirit causes the Christian to grow.

Such growth is fed by carefully reading and studying the Scriptures, and by faithfully obeying the voice of the Spirit. In this way, the Spirit leads us to give more and more of ourselves to God and God's cause on earth, to greater passion for what is right, and to a greater desire to share Christ with others.

All Christians recognize God as Creator, Revealer, Redeemer, and Sanctifier. As Sanctifier, God makes possible growth in holiness, in living that is good and whole and rooted in God, through the Word and the Spirit.

THE BIBLE

Christians believe the Bible is the written Word of God. The Spirit uses the Word of God to help us see our wrong ways and feel ready to turn toward the right ways the Bible illustrates.

An important way the Bible does this is by telling us stories of people like us. Some, like Samson, lived rightly for a time but then pulled death down on themselves by their inability to stay focused on God. Some, like Peter, were as weak, as uncertain about how to live coura-geously for God, as any of us. But they were transformed into rocklike people by God's pow-er.

Through such examples, we learn who we are, in all our imperfections. Then we are also chal-lenged to become all we could be if we let God's Spirit change us.

Through the Word, the Spirit also guides the Christian and causes him or her to grow in Christ. A key way the Bible does this is by giving us pictures of the way Christ lived.

When we see Christ drawing power, not sim-ply from limited human resources, but from God, we too feel ourselves invited to live like that. We are stirred to live for God even when opposed, as did Christ. And we are strength-ened by the Bible's promise that the Christ who lived then remains with us always, "even unto the end of the age."

Christians believe the Bible was written by holy people of God, mostly the prophets of Isra-el and the apostles of Christ (including Paul). The Bible bears the marks of true humanity on every page, including the viewpoints held by God's people in the various parts of its writing.

Yet it is also the inspired and trustworthy Word of God, able to guide us to God through Christ. It is the handbook of the Christian church and the manual of faith, obedience, love, and right living for the Christian.

SALVATION THROUGH FAITH

Christians who are by God's mercy and grace "in Christ" speak of having salvation or of being saved. Salvation means being at peace with God through Jesus Christ. It means that when God comes into the garden of our lives as God did after Adam and Eve sinned, we no longer run and hide, because now our friendship with God has been restored.

Salvation comes for any who turn away from their wrong ways toward Jesus Christ and thus receive God's forgiveness. We receive from God the gift of righteousness—we are "righteous by faith." This simply means we are made right with God.

Indeed, the gospel of the New Testament is the good news that God is ready to forgive and accept all who have faith in Christ.

God does this because Christ's sacrifice on the cross of Golgotha, outside Jerusalem on Good Friday, frees us from sin and death. God can raise us to new life, just as God raised Jesus from the dead that first Easter morning (AD 30).

THE CHURCH

Those who respond to the good news by turning from sin toward faith in Jesus love to connect with each other. We call this the church or assembly of God and of Christ. We think of those who belong to God as a body of Christ.

We also speak of the church as the people of

God or the new Israel of God, the new humanity. The church is even called the "bride" of Christ, for it has made and is making a surrender of love and trust to Christ.

The church is that community of people who have chosen to follow Jesus' way and not the world's way. It is those disciples who band together to help each other live according to the Bible and not only by the rules of societies which are often falling apart.

When the church is faithful, it shows the violent, the divided, the oppressive, and the racist what living that is peaceful, whole, just, and open to all people can look like.

PRAYER

The Bible teaches Christians to pray "in the name of Christ." Because believers are in Christ and pray through him, they know that God hears and answers their prayers. God may not always answer the way we would like. But God doesn't turn a deaf ear to us.

Here are a few of the things for which Christians pray: for greater ability to live rightly, divine guidance, daily cleansing from sin; for blessings on God's kingdom on earth and those who are a part of it; for daily needs, healing from worry, anxiety, hatred, envy, grudges, and broken or marred relationships; and for physical healing.

LIVING THAT CENTERS ON GOD

Christians believe that saving faith in God through Jesus Christ involves centering one's heart and life on God and living out the results of such centering. Saving faith also requires obedience to the will of God as shown in the Word and as lived and taught by Jesus.

This faith provides spiritual security through the gracious care of a heavenly Parent. God provides for our every need by giving us the Holy Spirit to strengthen and guide us.

WORSHIP

Christians believe God wants us to worship God "in the Spirit," both in private and in groups. God is God—and as Creator and Sustainer of the universe, God deserves our worship. Christians are weak because of their human nature (that part of us which continually seems to want to twist away from God and toward our own self-centered drives).

We need worship to be strengthened. We need it to be reminded of whom and whose we are. We need it to learn—as did Abram who became Abraham, Jacob who became Israel, Simon who became Peter—what new names God wants to give us.

CHRIST'S RETURN

The final hope of the church is the second coming of Christ. At the end of history, Christ will come a second time, not to die for sin again, but to show that all the world's suffering has finally been made right. On that day, God will raise the dead, judge the world, and make complete that kingdom whose firstfruits we now taste wherever faithful living is present. On that day the old things will pass away, and God will dry our tears.

NEED OF SALVATION

Christians believe that all of us are sinners before God. That is, all have sinned and fall short of the standard of life God has outlined in the Bible. All of us, therefore, need a savior to deliver us from the guilt and the power of sin.

Since we could not provide such a deliverer, God bridged the gap separating humans from God. God sent Jesus to die as a sacrifice for sin. Christ's death takes away the guilt of sin, reconciles us to God, and breaks the power of sin.

In short, Christ's death makes it possible for all to receive deliverance and well-being, called *salvation* in the New Testament. To be delivered, we must hear the gospel, turn from sin, and put our trust in Christ who loved us and died for us. This then can empower us to offer a suffering, frightened, doubting world the good news of God's liberating plans.

TWO

How the Sixteenth Century Affects People Today

During the Middle Ages, the light of Christ's teaching flickered in Christendom. The church had in part moved away from its New Testament base. It needed to be renewed and reformed. In the beginning of the sixteenth century, all professing Christians were expected to be members of the "Holy Catholic Church." Here we will speak of this church as the Church of Tradition.

23

Today, although scars remain, numerous people on both sides of the rupture described below are learning to work together instead of against each other. Back then, however, the break many Christians made with the Church of Tradition was a harsh one. It has colored (sometimes unfairly) the way those who left it have viewed the Church of Tradition.

A BREAK WITH TRADITION

In the view of those who broke away, the Church of Tradition thought it unnecessary to be converted and born again spiritually to become sons and daughters of God.

The Church considered the seven sacraments powerful channels of God's grace. God had given the priests the power to change the communion wafer (bread) into the very body and blood of the Lord.

Thus, faithful members of the true Roman Catholic Church supposedly could literally eat Christ to save their souls. The church also added many holy ceremonies, beyond the seven sacraments, to meet every human need.

People were taught to believe that many persons in heaven stood ready to hear the prayers directed to them. In addition to God, Jesus, and the Holy Spirit, this included angels, departed saints, apostles, and martyrs—and Mary, the Blessed Virgin.

The church claimed power to release the dead

from purgatory, a place where they were thought to suffer for their sins before going to heaven. The church was believed to have power to store good deeds in a treasury of merits. It could then exchange these for the suffering the departed had earned because of sins.

The church also taught that it had power, through what were called *indulgences*, to draw on the good deeds stored in the treasury of merits. By doing so, it could spare people the agony of purgatory—even before the sin was committed.

THE CHURCH OF THE WORD

The Reformers of the sixteenth century sought to free the church from these doctrines and practices, which they considered unscriptural.

Luther and others like him in various countries of Europe sought to bring the church under the Word of God. These churches of the Word called for a return to the Bible as the only source of authority for the church.

These churches taught the awesome majesty and holiness of God. They saw the wonderful sacrifice of Jesus on the cross as more important than ceremonies. They regarded the good news of the gospel as of highest importance in the life and witness of God's people.

They taught, as did the New Testament, that only Christ can deliver from sin, for Christ has already made peace with God. Only Christ can overthrow the binding power of sin and Satan.

Each person must, however, by individual repentance and faith, allow the Savior to offer deliverance from sin and a new relationship with God. These churches of the Word insisted that only by the amazing grace of God can anyone be saved.

Rome, the seat of the pope, and Wittenberg, Luther's base, differed on the very nature of Christian truth. Rome said that the final authority for the church was Scripture and tradition. Luther and the other Reformers insisted it was only the Word of God.

A NEW TESTAMENT FAITH

The Reformers tried once more to establish churches of the Word. Some truths which the Reformers taught with great care are still taught by Mennonites today.

On God's part, salvation can be given only by grace. On the part of human beings, it can be accepted only by faith. All Christian doctrine and practice must rest firmly on the Word of Christ—Holy Scripture.

When Christians read and meditate on the Word of God, the Holy Spirit aids and blesses them. The Spirit helps them understand whatever is necessary for salvation and for a rich and meaningful Christian life.

When one is in Christ, a saved and forgiven believer, God fully accepts him or her. It is, therefore, unnecessary, and even offensive, to seek to satisfy God by good works or human self-denial. For example, some people refuse to eat certain foods at certain times of the year or do good deeds to try to win God's favor.

Now good deeds, or such rituals as fasting, can be helpful to the Christian life. But they are not what earn us God's love, which God freely gives us when we turn to God through faith in Jesus Christ.

The Reformers believed that Christians should live a normal life in society. This might include marriage, owning property, or serving in any honorable trade, profession, or occupation.

The Reformers were sharply opposed to the office of pope. They felt it vested too much authority in a human being, against which the New Testament warns.

The Reformers disagreed with the Roman Catholic view of the mass. They felt that the mass, which re-offered Jesus Christ on the cross daily in all the churches (transubstantiation) was a dishonor to Christ. His sacrifice for sin made on the cross so many centuries ago was and is sufficient.

TWO TRADITIONAL TEACHINGS

We have seen that there was a large body of Christian truth which was not lost during the Middle Ages. This truth was held in common by Catholics and by Anabaptist Mennonites.

We have also observed the work of the Reformers. One set of reformers, who came to be called Anabaptists (because they rebaptized adults, as will be explained later) went even further than the Reformers in the rediscovery of the gospel.

However, on two points the Anabaptists were closer to the teachings of the Roman Catholics than to the reforms of Luther.

First, the Anabaptists were not against nor afraid of doing good works. They saw them, however, not as ways to earn God's merit or friendship, but as the result of saving faith. An ancient Swiss writer says that the Anabaptists insisted on good works even more strongly than the Catholics did.

Second, the Anabaptists wanted to make Christ known wherever they could. They believed strongly in evangelism and outreach. They felt that every believer was commissioned by Christ and the church to be a witness.

The great commission is binding on Christians to the end of time, they held. Thus it is our duty to make disciples of all.

With this the Catholics agreed. The Lutheran theologians at that time, however, saw the great commission as binding only on the apostles of Christ and on the missionaries of the early church. They believed that the great commission was fulfilled in the apostolic age.

Therefore, it did not apply to European Christians of the sixteenth century, they thought. This was because everyone then was made a Christian through infant baptism or *christening*.

THREE

Just How Are Mennonites Different?

The Reformers and Anabaptists of the sixteenth century laid the foundation for the return to New Testament Christianity. From this renewal movement emerged a number of key concerns that Mennonites hold today.

THE NATURE OF THE CHURCH

A key concern of the Anabaptists was the nature

of the church and its place in society. Perhaps their most radical demand was that church and state must be separate.

Both the church and state, they held, were institutions of God. The state maintains law and order in a society which is largely unchristian.

It must, therefore, use law and the threat of force to restrain sinners. Thus, the officer of the state does not bear or wear the sword in vain. The Anabaptists believed that Romans 13 supported the use of force by the state.

The church, on the other hand, is a fellowship of love where men and women love the Lord and one another. Christians have a higher allegiance or authority than the law. They turn away from crime and sin because of an inner desire to please Christ, and not out of fear of punishment.

Their guideline for moral action is found in Romans 12. This Scripture passage tells us to present our bodies as a living sacrifice to God, just as Old Testament believers presented an offering to the Lord.

That is, we are to serve God because of the love provided for us through Christ's crucifixion. We are to be sincere in our love.

And this love is to be so great—and so contrary to normal human nature—that we can love even our enemies. This love will help enemies to believe in Christ as Savior.

As the Anabaptists read the Scriptures, they came to the conclusion that they were to be suffering, forgiving, loving followers of the Prince of Peace. They simply could not fill the law-enforcing, crime-suppressing role of the state.

They also firmly believed that to live out the teachings of Romans 12 they needed the love of God—as described in Romans 5:5—poured into their hearts. This love would draw them into a gathering of like-minded friends—the church.

Contrasts Between State and Church

In the Anabaptist-Mennonite tradition a number of contrasts appear between church and state. We enter the state by our natural birth. We enter the church by the new birth.

The state embraces all people, good and bad. The church is to be made up of those who are "walking in the resurrection" (as Michael Sattler, one Anabaptist leader, said it).

The function of the state includes maintaining law and order. The function of the church is evangelism and Christian nurture.

The state controls by law, by the sword, by the gun. The church depends upon the Word of God, the spiritual "sword," and the Spirit of God, to mold and guide its members.

The state may use fines and imprisonment, and in some cases even death, to control the behavior of its citizens. Whether all forms of control used by the state are blessed by God can be hotly debated. Does God, for example, bless the use of capital punishment? But whatever controls the state uses, the only formal means of control the church uses is excommunication.

The head of the state is a mere human being. The head of the church is the Lord Jesus Christ. The state comes to an end at the return of Christ. The church will *not* come to an end. It will enter the presence of God upon the return of Christ.

Many Catholics during the Middle Ages felt that the pope had two swords. With the sword of the Spirit (the Word of God), he "ruled" over the church. With the sword of steel, he ruled over the kings of the earth.

The latter view had to be dropped when the nations defeated the pope in war. Today the pope's rule extends over only the tiny Vatican City in Rome.

Most Protestant groups have believed that as individuals they should be kind and forgiving. But as citizens of the state, they can serve in the government, the police, and the military.

Most Christians, including the Anabaptists, regard government as a good gift of God, for God does not want chaos on the earth. Government is a divine institution.

However, the Anabaptists of Switzerland and Netherlands, now known as Mennonites, felt they had to withdraw from the law enforcement and war-waging functions of the state. They did so to follow both the letter and the spirit of the New Testament. They were the first peace church of modern times.

In the seventeenth century, the Society of Friends took a similar peace position. In the early eighteenth century, the German Baptists (Church of the Brethren since 1908) took their stand as the third peace church.

Withdrawal from personal involvement in violence has been one key approach of the peace churches. In modern times, some Mennonites and many other Christians have begun to doubt whether God wants even the state to use violence.

Church as Community
The Catholic Church of the Middle Ages had strict levels of authority. These ranged upward from the laity to priests, bishops, and so on. The pope was the bishop of the bishops.

Such hierarchy has made Mennonites uncomfortable. They have noted that Jesus told followers in Matthew 23:8-9 that they should make no use of titles such as rabbi or father, "for you have one teacher, and you are all brethren."

Jesus reminded the disciples that in the world of the nations the rulers rule over their subjects. But Jesus said that if anyone wished to be great, he or she should become a servant, even a slave (Matt. 20:25-27). In the kingdom of Christ, greatness means capacity to love and serve, not exercise of authority or honor and status.

Therefore, a minister is not to be set above others in the family of God. Rather, the minister is entrusted with the pastoral care of the congregation and is responsible to faithfully teach the Word. (See Jesus teaching about shepherds in John 10:1-16 and the apostle Peter's instruction in 1 Peter 5:1-7.)

It therefore seems proper to refer to all members of the church as brothers and sisters. In this view, giving leaders such titles as "reverend" is inappropriate.

In the same way, one member of Christ's body should not be considered more important than another because of wealth. In New Testament times, slaves who became members of the church were to rejoice that they had been elevated to serve Christ (Eph. 6:5-6; Col. 3:22; 1 Tim. 6:1).

Likewise the masters of the slaves were to remember that they and their slaves had a common Master (Eph. 6:9; Col. 4:1).

Christians must not value a person according to level of education. Wisdom can be received by every member of Christ's body, for the Holy Spirit gives wisdom to each member as he or she asks for it in faith. All members of the body of Christ are to show the mind of Christ.

The New Testament emphasis on a one-level family of God speaks with special authority in today's world of racial inequality. The members of each race must love, accept, and respect all other races, for we all belong to the one human race and have a common origin.

Out of Adam, God made all the nations of the earth (Acts 17:26). It is therefore a sin a look down on any person because of race or national background.

Christian Mutual Aid

The New Testament strongly encourages Christians to love and help each other: "As we have opportunity, let us do good to all men, and especially to those who are of the household of faith" (Gal. 6:10).

In the same epistle we are told, "Bear one another's burdens, and so fulfill the law of Christ" (Gal. 6:2).

Christ told us what his commandment was: "That you love one another as I have loved you" (John 15:12). Showing love to the one in need is really a test. "If any one . . . sees his brother in need, yet, closes his heart against him, how does God's love abide in him?" (1 John 3:17). A true Christian cannot be selfishly indifferent to the need of another person.

Mennonites in Switzerland and in the Netherlands, and later in Russia and North America, cared for the aged, the orphans, the handicapped, the sick, and the emotionally ill. Recently this caring concern has been extended to prisoners, refugees, and persons suffering from famine, fires, floods, tornadoes, and other natural disasters.

Mennonite Central Committee, commonly referred to as MCC, is a Mennonite organization that works at supplying food, clothing, and shelter for needy persons around the world. MCC also helps solve hunger and poverty through training and adaptation to local resources and conditions.

Mennonite Disaster Service (MDS), a special section of MCC, assists persons stricken by natural disasters to return to their homes.

Mennonite Economic Development Associates (MEDA) provides financial help to needy persons who want to start small businesses.

Many young people are now giving time to Voluntary Service (VS). They care for the sick, the aged, those with mental and physical disabilities, and the like.

Mennonites of North America have also set up an organization called Mennonite Mutual Aid (MMA) to offer hospital, medical, and other forms of insurance to the members of the church on a mutual sharing basis. Although rates are rising, as they are for all insurance companies, members have the satisfaction of helping brothers and sisters who are in need.

MMA is one way to practice the Christian principle of bearing one another's burdens. It is not merely a selfish desire to be covered should some health problem or other emergency arise.

Many areas of the church also have mutual aid associations which come to the aid of brothers and sisters when they suffer loss by fire, storm, or flood.

Christians in Colombia have learned to provide mutual assistance to each other. When Mrs. Garzon went to work, she left her young family at home alone. There was no money to pay someone to take care of them. The oldest daughter managed to look after the baby and other children.

One day, however, while she was lighting the kerosene stove to heat the baby's bottle, flames flared. The small house with all their possessions was destroyed. The children escaped safely.

Some former students of the Mennonite grade school in Cachipay, Columbia, heard about the loss. They were part of a larger group of alumni that met every Sunday for worship and sharing. Most struggled to pay their own expenses, but helping others was important to them. Soon money, clothing, food, furniture, and encouragement had been given to Mrs. Garzon.[1]

Church Organization

The church is the body of those who have been converted and have turned from sin to Christ, and in whom the Spirit of God dwells. The church is not officers, boards, committees, and other structures.

In the early church, people had a common faith in Christ and met for mutual strengthening and for the worship of God. They wanted to live a life worthy of Christ and share the joy caused by following Jesus.

Congregations

The Lord directed each congregation to have pastors, known as overseers or elders in the New Testament. These pastors were not on a different level from the other brothers and sisters of the congregations. Rather, after much prayer the church selected them, laid hands on them, and charged them to be faithful shepherds of the Lord's "flock."

These persons were often referred to as pastors, preachers, or ministers. They were to watch over the congregation and to feed the members with the rich food of the Word of God. Mennonite leadership styles are becoming more varied, but this is one key pattern Mennonites try to follow.

The New Testament also recognized pastoral assistants or deacons, as in Philippians 1:1. The spiritual gifts required of overseers and deacons are given in 1 Timothy 3. (The *bishop* of the King James Version is better translated *overseer* because of the prestige and power which have been attached to the word bishop in church history.) The overseers have two main responsibilities. They are to oversee the work of the pastors and carry out a teaching ministry.

Historically, the *deacons* served in what might be called general welfare. They helped to maintain a state of happiness and peace in the congregation. They looked after any financial needs, especially among orphans and widows. Women such as Phoebe probably served as deaconesses in the congregations (Rom. 16:1).

Here is an example of a good deacon. In a Mennonite congregation, a young widow with four children was running out of food and fuel. She did not tell her children that they had eaten the last food in the house for their evening meal.

Since she had fuel for only one more day, she moved the children's beds into the kitchen where it was warm. Then she lovingly put them to bed for the night. After they were asleep, she knelt and poured out her heart to God in prayer. She knew God could see her plight.

As she prayed, a feeling of deep peace came upon her. So she too retired for the night and slept soundly.

At four in the morning, she was awakened by someone knocking at the door. She opened it. Her deacon stood outside. He told her that he had gotten awake at midnight and could not sleep because she was on his mind.

"I felt led to bring you a load of fuel and food," he said.

He then began to carry the food into the house and to unload the fuel. The widow's heart sang for joy. She had discovered how faithfully God supplies our needs—and that God does so through other people.

District Conferences and General Assembly
Church organization beyond each congregation includes the district conferences. These are fellowships of ministers and delegates chosen by congregations. Pastors and delegates come together to affirm one another, to help each other face problems, and to consider how to best build up the congregations in the faith.

The General Assembly of the Mennonite Church has the same kind of function, only it represents all the congregations of the denomination in North America.

Program Boards
The five program boards of the Mennonite Church are service organizations. The Mission Board directs the mission work of the church. It looks for workers, arranges their transportation, and receives money for their support.

The Publication Board oversees a publishing house and book stores. It provides for the literature needs of the church.

The Education Board helps guide the schools, colleges, and seminaries of the church as they meet the church's need for Christian education.

The Board of Congregational Ministries helps congregations and their pastors become more effective in carrying out their various ministries.

The Mutual Aid Board provides systematic care for those who have needs which ought to be shared by the brotherhood.

The exact pattern of boards and committees varies from one group of Mennonites to another and from one country to another. Conferences and boards help organizations provide needed services. The essence of the church is always faith and life in Christ, not structure.

SYMBOLIC CHURCH CEREMONIES

Several ceremonies practiced by the Mennonite Church symbolize for believers their faith and life in Jesus Christ. These include water baptism of believers only (in contrast to infant baptism), the Lord's Supper, and foot washing.

Water Baptism

We find a sharp contrast in the New Testament between the outer sign of water baptism and the inner reality to which it points. This inner reality is Christ's baptism with the Spirit. (See Matt. 3:11; Mark 1:8; Luke 3:16; John 1:33; Acts 1:5; and 1 Cor. 12:13).

Mennonites believe that water baptism does not magically call the Holy Spirit into the life of a believer. But it is a way the Christian shows commitment to God through Jesus and opens his or her heart to the presence of the Spirit.

What are some of the signs or pictures water baptism offers? We see baptism as a picture of divine cleansing from sin. Water is frequently used for cleansing. The New Testament speaks of water baptism as if it removes the stains of sin.

In one of the accounts of Paul's conversion, God's servant Ananias told the blind convert from the Damascus road: "Receive your sight . . . . And now why do you wait? Rise and be baptized, and wash away your sins, calling on his name" (Acts 22:13,16).

Of course, Paul could not wash away his sins. But if he met the conditions, he could receive this divine cleansing which Christ accomplishes by "inner baptism." The meaning of the passage seems to be: "See to it that your sins get washed away."

We also believe that water baptism stands for our death to sin and our resurrection to new life in Christ. Romans 6 tells us why we are now "dead" to sin: When we were baptized, we were baptized into the death of Christ. Christ was literally crucified, put to death, and buried.

Spiritually, our break with sin is to be equally clear and final. If we translate the original Greek literally, it says that as we are co-crucified, we are to co-live with Christ.

The apostle Paul in Ephesians 2 picks up the same thought. He says that we were co-quickened (made alive) with Christ, co-raised (ascended) with Christ, and co-seated with Christ in heaven (vv. 5-6).

This simply means that when we repent and believe in Christ through the power of the Holy Spirit, we turn our backs on sin as if we had died—as did Jesus. Our water baptism symbolizes this death.

Our new life in Christ is as miraculous as if we had literally risen from the dead. We testify that Christ has done this miracle in us when we ask for water baptism.

The apostle Paul says, "If then you have been [co-raised] with Christ, seek the things that are above, where Christ is, seated at the right hand of God" (Col. 3: 1). The person to be baptized promises to die to sin and to the old life of Satan.

In the power of the Spirit of God, the person can do this. If God can make a dead person come to life, God can make a weak person (the Christian) walk in victory. This victory truth is celebrated in water baptism.

The key thought in 1 Peter 3:18-21 is that Christ died once for all on the cross for our sins. Christ, who was tested and tempted as we are but did not yield to sin, died for us, who do yield. The purpose of his death was to bring us into a relationship with God. Water baptism is the pledge or covenant of a good conscience with God given through the resurrection of Christ.

Thus water baptism is not for the actual washing of the body. Rather, it is a pledge to God. We can make this pledge only because through Christ we can draw on the same power of the Spirit that filled Christ. As the Spirit empowered Christ to resist temptation and raised him from the dead, so can it let us walk as true disciples.

The baptism of Jesus, which marks the beginning of his public ministry, is recorded in Matthew 3:13, Mark 1:9, and Luke 3:21. When Jesus was baptized with water, the Holy Spirit came down on him in the form of a dove, and God spoke words of approval.

Jesus was prepared by the Spirit to begin his teaching ministry. On the day of baptism, Christ started down the road which led to the cross. Through water baptism, Jesus declared himself ready to pay the price of faithfully doing the will of God as God's witness on earth.

We Christians are to walk as Christ walked. We are to identify with him in our baptism. We thereby declare that we are ready to begin our mission as believers. We show that we want to be faithful witnesses for our Lord.

To Mennonites, therefore, baptism is once again a witness to our baptism by the Holy Spirit. It is this which lets us witness to Christ and the good news of the gospel.

The followers of Conrad Grebel and Felix Manz in Zurich, Switzerland, stood up for believers baptism.

They did this at first as disciples of reformer Huldrich Zwingli, who in 1523 was calling for believers baptism. He then thought that the fourth-century system of baptizing believers would be more desirable than christening infants.

Later Zwingli decided to cling to infant baptism. Grebel and his friends continued to study the Word, and in 1524, Grebel argued persuasively for believers baptism.

In 1525, a number of Grebel's followers were rebaptized on the basis of their belief and commitment to Christ. Zwingli and the state church named these rebaptized believers *Anabaptists*, which meant rebaptizers. The Anabaptists thus broke away from the state church. They were later named free churchpeople.

Zwingli and other sixteenth-century Reformers accused the Anabaptists of damning the infants by refusing to baptize them. The Anabaptists rejected this charge. Because of the testimony of Scripture, the free churchpeople simply could not bring themselves to believe that infants will be damned.

The Bible nowhere says that unbaptized infants are lost or that they are denied the presence of God in a "limbo" should they die. The Bible says "God is love" (1 John 4:16).

Romans 5 indicates that, although the human race was condemned through Adam's sin, it is returned to God's favor through Christ. His sacrifice is adequate for all, is offered to all, and is intended for all. Just as there was oneness in sin and death, so now there is oneness in a right standing with God through life in Christ.

Infants are a part of the human race for whom Christ died. His sacrifice was adequate and covers their sin until they become aware of and responsible to accept Christ's saving work. Infants are spiritually safe.

In Mark 10:14 Jesus used the example of children to show what the kingdom of God is like. He said, "Let the children come to me, do not hinder them; for to such belongs the kingdom of God."

When Jesus was asked who might be the greatest in the kingdom, he stood a child before him as an example (Matt. 18:1-5). It is therefore right to give children nurture. It is right to teach them about God and the new life offered through Christ, to teach them that God watches over us, even to teach them that God forgives our sins for Christ's sake.

But children cannot be evangelized, for they are not lost. As a child grows, the Lord knows when to call that individual to repentance, new life, and commitment to Jesus as Savior and Lord. Readiness for this commitment is often called the "age of accountability." Mennonite young people are often baptized in their teen years, but always their request.

The Lord's Supper
The New Testament contains four references to the beginning of the Lord's Supper: Matthew 26, Mark 14, Luke 22, and 1 Corinthians 11.

On the first day of the Festival of Unleavened Bread (Passover Week), Jesus sent two disciples to prepare for the Passover meal in a private home in Jerusalem. During the meal that evening, Jesus told his disciples plainly that he wanted to eat this meal with them before he suffered.

The Passover was observed as a memorial of Israel's deliverance from slavery in Egypt. The death of the firstborn in each Egyptian home made Pharaoh thrust Israel out of his land. But God had instructed the Israelites to kill a lamb. They were to smear the blood of the lamb on the lintels and doorposts of their homes. God told them, "When I see the blood, I will pass over you." God would thus spare their firstborn.

Now Jesus himself was about to become the Passover lamb, slain "once for all." Now Jesus would provide atonement for, or cleansing of, sins. Because of the believer's faith in Christ's cleansing blood, God will now "pass over" our sins.

Jesus wanted to eat this Passover and give the disciples a new memorial meal to recall his sacrifice for sin. As Jesus was eating the Passover meal, he took bread, gave thanks to God, broke it, and shared it with the twelve. "This is my body which is given for you," he said. "Do this in remembrance of me." Likewise Jesus took the cup and said, "This cup . . . is the new covenant in my blood."

By these simple words, Jesus set up his sacred and deeply significant memorial of his body which was about to be broken and his blood which was about to be shed. Through his death, he would make a total sacrifice for human sin for all time. With few exceptions, the Christian church has been faithful in observing this Lord's Supper.

In the New Testament, the bread is spoken of as a loaf which symbolized the spiritual unity of those in Christ. This was a major emphasis of the Swiss Brethren, as the first Anabaptists came to be known in their homeland.

Before coming to the Lord's table, they insisted that each participant must be brought into one body in Christ by believers baptism. They also taught that any offenses between members of the church must be cleared up and full reconciliation made before sharing in the communion service.

Mennonites have partly departed from the faith of their founders in the mood in which people celebrate the Lord's Supper. Menno Simons, for example, thought Supper should be taken with holy joy. In time the service became so solemn as to be somber and heavy, with people often wearing dark clothes. Now the mood is perhaps swinging at least partway back to Menno.

Foot Washing—A Symbol of Peoplehood

Throughout his ministry Jesus tried to teach his followers to give no thought to status and prestige. But the night before he went to the cross, a dispute broke out among the twelve as to who was the greatest (Luke 22:24-27).

Jesus rebuked the disciples by demonstrating his teaching about love and equality. During the solemn Passover meal, he arose from supper and laid aside his outer garments. Then he girded himself with a towel, and began to wash the feet of the twelve (John 13).

Today we can hardly grasp how out of place this seemed to the twelve disciples. Ashamed, Peter told Jesus not to wash his feet. Jesus then explained the real cleansing of heart which he needed to give them.

After hearing this, Peter wanted his hands and head washed as well! The climax came in the words of Jesus: "If I then, your Lord and Teacher, have washed your feet, you also ought to wash one another's feet. For I have given you an example, that you also should do as I have done to you" (John 13:14-15).

The early Christian church was not certain how to understand this command of Jesus to wash one another's feet. Did he mean only that they should serve one another in love? Many Christians thought so.

On the other hand, Tertullian (about AD 200) thought that foot washing should be practiced as Jesus taught and observed it. Ambrose, bishop of Milan in the fourth century, as well as Augustine (354-430), wrote of its literal observance.

The most remarkable rule was made at the

Synod of Toledo in AD 694—foot washing was to be literally observed on the Thursday before Good Friday. Further, foot washing was required before coming to the Lord's table to celebrate communion. Bernard of Clairvaux (1091-1153) saw the ceremony as a symbol of the Christian's daily cleansing.

Balthasar Hubmaier, martyred in 1528, seems to be the first Anabaptist to have practiced the washing of the saints' feet (1525). The best explanation of the ceremony was made by Dirk Philips, a colleague of Menno Simons. Dirk saw it as a symbol or picture of Christ's continuing cleansing of the believer and of the Christian esteem we have for our fellow saints.

The observance of foot washing among the Dutch Mennonites began with the Danziger Old Flemish. They practiced it as a house ceremony to be given to the elders. It was attached to the Lord's Supper by the Old Flemish about the year 1588. The Amish began observing it after 1693. However, the Mennonites in Switzerland did not observe it literally.

Among Mennonites in North America, pairs of brothers in the faith and pairs of sisters wash each others' feet and greet one another with a holy kiss and a spoken blessing in Christ. The practice has waxed and waned. Currently, after fading in many congregations, it seems to be undergoing a revival. The ceremony remains a powerful picture of equality and servanthood in a world where people have largely forgotten how to serve each other.

IMPORTANT ASPECTS OF CHURCH LIFE

From the beginning Mennonites have believed that Christians should help each other to do what pleases, rather than dishonors, God. In practice, this is called church discipline. Let's look at how the Anabaptists understood discipline.

Church Discipline

The word *discipline* should not be thought of as punishment. It means affirmation, encouragement, and correction given in love to other members of the church. Discipline in the church has to do with helping people become more faithful, effective witnesses and disciples.

The true believer does not anything to destroy the good name of Christ and Christ's cause. Believers need each other's help to become more faithful disciples of the cross-bearing Savior.

An important passage on this subject for the Anabaptists was Matthew 18, along with Romans 12. Jesus told us in Matthew 18:15 that if we see someone sin, we should go and set him or her on the right path again. By doing this, we prevent a more serious falling away from the faith.

Galatians 6:1 underscores this concern, saying

that those who are spiritual should restore one who has sinned in a spirit of gentleness. "Look to yourself, lest you too be tempted," it concludes.

The concerned member of the body of Christ does not approach the one in momentary defeat with a proud, accusing spirit. Rather, one goes in a spirit of humility and deep caring, knowing how easy it is to fall into sin.

The Christian speaks words of affirmation and encouragement in love to help restore an erring brother or sister to fellowship again, rather than crushing them into humiliation. If we lack such a heart of genuine, caring love, we would do well to allow someone else to restore the person!

New Testament church discipline seeks to maintain holiness and a clean life before the Lord in the body of Christ rather than to keep up some long-established set of rules. The saints do need one another in their task of "binding and loosing" (Matt. 18:18; John 20:23). That is, the church using the Word of God binds the sins of the unrepentant to them. It releases those who repent from their guilt.

The witness of the church is effective when Spirit-led Christians agree on their stand against the sins of their society, such as taking advantage of the poor or treating persons unjustly because of race or sex. Such a witness is often referred to as the prophetic witness of the church.

By disciplining such sins in the church, the

church lays a foundation for an effective witness against such sins in society.

Witnessing

"You will be my witnesses," said Jesus to his disciples shortly before the ascension (when he physically left earth to be with God). The King James Version might give the modern reader the impression that this is a command. But it is better understood as a statement of fact.

In other words, the Lord meant that the Holy Spirit will fill Christians with such love, such joy, such passion that people will be drawn to the Savior. They will so hunger to possess the Christian's love, joy, and peace that they too will turn from sin to the Lord.

Being filled with the Spirit creates a desire in the believer to share the good news of the gospel with those who do not yet know Christ.

When the early Christians remained at home in Jerusalem, the Lord allowed persecution to fall on them. Thus, they were scattered far and wide.

Wherever they went, they shared the good news. The earliest mission churches were established in this way by Paul, Barnabas, Silas, and others.

Paul started with the Gentile "proselytes of the gate." These were non-Israelites who enjoyed worshiping with the Jews. They would listen to the Scriptures and to the teaching of the synagogue leaders about God and the coming Christ.

In many cases, Jews who refused to believe that Jesus was the Messiah drove Paul out. Yet many Gentiles and some Jews followed Paul into the new Christian "synagogue" or church he established.

In the first 150 years of the Christian church, many people turned to the Lord in those countries bordering the Mediterranean Sea. These included the present Turkey, Greece, Italy, France, South Germany, and North Africa. Before long the Christian faith had spread all the way to the British Isles.

It was also carried through Persia all the way to India—if the Christians of South India know their history. By AD 1000, all of Europe more or less considered itself Christian, although the Christianity of that era was not fully biblical. Most Christians by that time felt that the great commission was no longer relevant.

The rise of Anabaptists of the sixteenth century renewed interest in Christ's Great Commission. These radical reformers in Switzerland, Moravia, Germany, and the Netherlands, began to share their New Testament understandings with great vigor.

Before long the state churches of that time persuaded the governments to persecute and kill many of the Anabaptists. During the first year of the movement, the Swiss Brethren seem to have had several dozen tiny congregations in the cantons of Zurich and Bern. But their leaders were soon silenced.

Conrad Grebel's itinerant ministry was cut short by the plague, which took his life the summer of 1526. The early Anabaptist leader-martyr, Felix Manz, was drowned in the Limmat River in Zurich early in 1527. Michael Sattler, an important Anabaptist thinker and writer, was tied to a stake and burned to death in May 1527.

So it was with one Anabaptist after another. The religious martyr ballads of the old Swiss hymnal, the *Ausbund* (from which the Amish still sing), tell of many of these witnesses who died because of their unusual obedience to New Testament Christianity.

An Example

One of the most effective witnesses was Hans Hut. He was born about 1490 and lived in the district called Franconia, in South Germany. He was a sexton or grounds keeper for a rich man from 1513 to 1517. Then he traveled about selling Lutheran books.

About the year 1524, he encountered Anabaptist ideas. He came to believe that baptism should be offered only to converted believers, those who had made an adult decision to follow Christ.

He also became disturbed at the low morals of some who had outwardly turned to the Lutheran faith. He seems also to have come into contact with the violent revolutionary, Thomas Muentzer. Finally, he came in contact with peaceful Anabaptism, was attracted to it, and accepted believers baptism in 1526.

Hut then began a remarkable evangelistic ministry, preaching wherever he could. He would stroll around in a city and invite people to come outside the town to a meeting to be held under a bridge or in the forest that evening. Sometimes several hundred persons gathered.

Hut would then preach from a passage such as Mark 16:15-16 "Go into all the world and preach the gospel to the whole creation. He who believes and is baptized will be saved." Many who heard him turned to Christ in faith.

Hut's theology and preaching were strongly Christ-centered. He believed baptism is for those who are ready to undertake the commitments and responsibilities of baptism.

He believed baptism should follow repentance and that it had a threefold meaning:

1. Baptism with the Spirit occurs when we make a covenant with Christ in our hearts;

2. Water baptism is a sign of the covenant that we make to live in obedience to our Lord;

3. The baptism of blood means readiness to suffer for Christ, even unto death.

Hut also taught mutual discipline in the church. Believers shall address the careless member who sins and refuses to walk in love.

Like all Anabaptists, he saw the Lord's Supper as a holy memorial to the suffering and death of Jesus Christ.

Hut died after horrible torture on December 6, 1527. His body was burned the next day as that of a heretic. Among his writings are *The Secret of Baptism*; *The Interpretation of Scripture*; a letter addressed *To All Good-hearted Christians*; and a catechism, *The Booklet of Counsel*. He also wrote a number of hymns.

CHRISTIAN EXPERIENCE
Defeatism Rejected

The severest criticism the Anabaptist made against the state church—Catholic or Protestant—was that their members did not walk in holiness; they did not care about right living.

Indeed, said the Anabaptist, the state church taught a theology of defeatism. "No one, they say, can live above sin. We are all sinners in thought, word, and deed. To claim to walk in holiness is fanaticism pure and simple."

No, holiness is not fanaticism, said the Anabaptists. It is the New Testament interpretation of the cross and of the resurrection of the Lord.

A Swiss Brethren minister, Martin Weniger, wrote a *Vindication* of Anabaptism in 1535. This document protests the theology of defeatism taught by the Protestant state church leaders of Switzerland. That no one can live in spiritual victory is simply not true, said Weniger. By living in Christ and being empowered by the Spirit, we can walk in victory over the world, the flesh, and the devil.

The works of Spirit-filled Christians are not displeasing to God! On the contrary, asserted Weniger, "The right done from the fear of the Almighty is pleasing to God."

The Anabaptists dared to believe the New Testament teaching that in our conversion we die to sin with our Lord and rise with him. Thus, we can, through the Spirit, "walk in the resurrection," as Michael Sattler described those who qualify for water baptism.

Spiritually, we rise with Christ to our real home in heaven. As we yield to the Lord through the Spirit, we even co-reign with, or become rulers with, Christ.

If we by the Spirit, not in human strength, kill the deeds of the flesh, we shall live—that is, we shall enjoy eternal life (Rom. 8:3). In the New Testament sense, all Christians should be holy.

No one denies, of course, that in themselves Christians are weak and imperfect. Victory comes through living in continuing surrender to Christ through the Spirit. This surrender does not necessarily happen instantly but can take a lifetime.

Christians must continue to grow in grace and in their knowledge of or acquaintance with Christ their Lord. When Christians fall short of their intentions, God extends grace to forgive their involuntary shortcomings.

Some people do claim to be more holy or perfect than they really are. Mennonites have sometimes fallen into this trap and then become legalists, people who care more about rules than relating to God.

However, in a time when a passion for right living is often missing, the more common mistake is not to claim the victory which is available in Christ to converted, Spirit-filled believers.

We then avoid legalism by realizing that we journey toward holiness without fully reaching it in this life—even as victory over sin remains our goal.

Divine Love "Poured In"
We cannot live the teaching of the New Testament in our own strength. It is not natural to human nature to forgive wrongdoing, to drop grudges, to continue to love when someone betrays a trust.

Therefore God through the Holy Spirit pours love into our hearts (Rom. 5:5). This divine love enables Christians to forgive, to show love when it is not deserved, to continue to hope for the best when disappointed, to return good for evil.

The New Testament does not tell us at what point or moment this divine love is received. Rather, it is an ongoing reality that we take hold of by faith day by day.

The New Testament does not describe one "experience" or formula which will guarantee perfect victory. It does not tell us how to live with no temptations and no struggles.

Rather, victory in all areas of life is to be claimed continuously by faith throughout the Christian life. Divine help and grace will always be needed to walk in love and holiness. We need all of God's grace and love to "walk in the resurrection."

Growth Through Grace

There is no neat formula for Christian growth. However, here are some activities and attitudes which those wanting to grow as Christians have often recommended:

1. To desire to do what God wants one to do continually;

2. To read and meditate frequently on the Scriptures;

3. To pray at all times, not only about needs, but praising and thanking God as well;

4. To look to the Lord for open doors to share Christ's salvation with others;

5. To fellowship with other believers;

6. To join in public worship services;

7. To promptly reject those impulses of the world, human nature, and the devil which tempt us to think or do what we know God is against;

8. To daily thank God for calling us into the kingdom, for giving us many blessings, and for continuing to forgive our sins and shortcomings;

9. To practice faithful, sacrificial, and generous stewardship—giving our money, time, and energy for God's sake;

10. To do good in every way possible—showing kindness to the miserable, forgiving those difficult to be with, and witnessing to those who can do something about the injustices of our society;

11. To live a well-managed life, with a proper balance between work, rest, recreation, suitable eating habits, using as little medicine as possible;

12. To trust God continually for safekeeping and for leading us in service.

These are not to be practiced as laws. We can see them as "means of grace," as habits through which God helps us mature.

THE CHRISTIAN LIFE

Christ is Our Lord

A difficult struggle emerged in the sixteenth century because the age of religious toleration had not yet dawned. State and church were actually united in the territorial churches of the era.

The system functioned with the Latin formula *Cujus regio, ejus religio* (Whose the region, his the religion). That is, the prince ordered his subjects to profess or agree to a particular religion.

The Anabaptists protested long and loud against this unscriptural practice. The Dutch

Anabaptist leader, Menno Simons, appealed to magistrates for religious toleration.

Menno believed that only God, or Christ, is the Lord of the conscience. The state has no right to dabble in matters of conscience. The church must be a free church, not controlled by the state.

Churches around the world still struggle with this issue. In some areas the church is almost free from government interference or control. In other areas the state tries to control the church in great detail.

As we deal with this tension in the nations in which we live, Mennonites try to follow the Word of God as guide.

The Obedience of Faith

The Anabaptists tried to obey not only the Ten Commandments and the Sermon on the Mount. They also searched the Word carefully and sought to avoid the error of "selective obedience," picking and choosing what they liked and rejecting what they disliked.

They tried earnestly to obey the instructions of Christ and the apostles—not to gain favor with God, but to please their Lord. The first Anabaptist, Conrad Grebel, wrote that "the doctrine of the Lord and his commandments have been given for the purpose of being carried out and put into practice."

The Anabaptists were accused again and

again of trying to get to heaven on their obedience only. They were falsely called "work-saints," "heaven-stormers," and other such names.

Yet some fine testimonies came from opponents of the Anabaptists. For example, a Catholic scholar, Franz Agricola, wrote in 1582,

> Among the existing heretical sects there is none which in appearance leads a more modest, better, or more pious life than the Anabaptists. As concerns their outward public life, they are irreproachable: no lying, deception, swearing, harsh language; no intemperate eating and drinking; no outward personal display is found among them, but humility, patience, uprightness, meekness, honesty, temperance, straightforwardness in such measure that one would suppose they have the Holy Spirit of God.

Many similar statements could be quoted. This does not mean that only the Mennonites (or all) lived in obedience to the Word of God. It does mean that their obedience in the sixteenth century was unusual enough for various observers to notice it.

Obedience to the "Hard Sayings"

The Mennonites also took at face value the so-called "hard sayings" of Jesus.

Jesus told his followers to avoid going to court, to settle disagreements out of court. What did he mean? Most Christians, even commentators, argue that he meant only to tell us not to be scrappy people, quick to run to court and the like.The Mennonites and several other groups, however, felt that Christ meant exactly what he said—we are not to sue each other.

The Old Testament was seen as a less complete revelation of the will of God. Many of Jesus' teachings are more strict than the Old Testament—such as the Old Testament's tolerance of an easy divorce system (Matt. 19:3-9).

Jesus' teaching in Matthew 5:25-26 against going to court is enlarged on in 1 Corinthians 6. These Scriptures gave the Anabaptists the confidence that they were rightly understanding the Master Teacher.

But perhaps Christ has an even more important teaching in mind—that we are not to be so attached to our possessions that we must go to court over them.

For example, Yakob of Tanzania owned a car that he often used as a taxi. He helped many people in his community with the car. One day he took his car to the garage of an Asian to have it greased. Then Yakob went on an errand.

The Indian garage owner had an African teenager who greased the cars. This teenager had never driven a car, but he loved cars and longed for a chance to drive one. He thought he knew how.

When nobody was looking, the teenager got

behind the wheel of Yakob's car and started out. He took it down the street but didn't know how to handle it. Before anyone could help him, he crashed the car into a deep ditch. It was badly wrecked.

Yakob came back to the garage and asked, "Where's my car?"

"Oh," the garage man said, "the boy must have taken it somewhere."

Just then a man came running down the street. He said, "I saw your car in a ditch around the corner."

Sure enough, Yakob found his car badly wrecked. The garage man and Yakob looked at it. The garage owner said, "I'll fix it for you." But he was trembling inside.

A policeman standing nearby said, "Yakob, take him to court; you can make him buy you a new car."

But Yakob said to the policeman, "I couldn't do that. The garage man said he would fix it. That is enough. The owner didn't wreck it, and I forgive the boy. Jesus will help me to do this."

The garage man fixed Yakob's car, and it ran very well. Yakob was satisfied.[2]

Many of us, including Christians and even some Mennonites, now sue each other regularly. One Mennonite recently had to decide whether to host a summer playgroup for his and ten other children in his home. Most of the other parents declined because they feared being sued if any child got hurt.

Imagine how much gentler we would become if we worked at settling our differences out of court instead of slapping each other with gigantic lawsuits!

Jesus also told his disciples that *they were not to swear*. They were not, for instance, to engage in the modern courtroom practice of solemnly swearing (on a Bible, no less), to tell only the truth and nothing but the truth. (Matt. 23:16-22). This is why today Mennonites simply *affirm* their commitment to tell the truth. Not swearing, said Jesus, is a recognition of our creaturehood, of our human limitations. We cannot even do such a tiny thing as make one hair grow white or black.

So, Jesus seems to be saying, admit your limitations and simply affirm your intention to tell the truth as far as it is possible for you. Jesus is saying that there is no need to try to strengthen or defend our witness by swearing (Matt. 5:33-37). James 5:12 gives the same instruction.

Another hard saying of Jesus is that *we are not to resist evildoers*. The Old Testament allowed a man to go to court and report the evil which his neighbor did to him.

According to the code then, the judge imposed on the evildoer the same suffering the evildoer had brought upon the injured man. The judge's manual read: life for life, eye for eye, tooth for tooth, hand for hand, burn for burn, wound for wound, stripe for stripe.

These words never meant that an injured Israelite get revenge by taking the law into his own hands. He was to report to the judges, and the judges were to impose sentence according to the formula of equal suffering.

Jesus also *opposed taking revenge* on someone who wrongs us. He even taught us not to use the law to retaliate and get even. Through the ministry of the Holy Spirit, our love for others should be so great that we do not retaliate at all. When struck, we shall turn the other cheek.

If someone tries—even by legal means—to take our shirt, we shall voluntarily surrender our coat also (Matt. 5:38-42). Give when someone is in need, and respond according to the law of love when someone wants to borrow from you.

Mennonites believed they should give up even their lives if necessary rather than kill another. This shapes their response to such complex current issues as nuclear warfare. How, they wonder, can we Christians hear Jesus ask us to turn the other cheek and then in any way support building, using, or even threatening to use nuclear weapons?

In Matthew 23:8-12 Jesus *warned against demanding titles of honor*, like rabbi (teacher) and father. This hard saying is difficult to carry out. Today we hear titles such as reverend, doctor, your lordship, and many more. Jesus tells us to avoid such titles. Be content to be addressed simply by name.

To obey this hard saying of Jesus, we have used New Testament words like brother and sister, even for persons called to serve as pastors, deacons, and overseers. We have tried to make the church a loving family of brothers and sisters rather than a place of status and honor.

In the Sermon on the Mount, in Matthew 6:19, Jesus *warned against storing up treasures on earth.* Earthly treasures can easily be lost or attacked by moth or rust. Jesus wants us to invest in the cause of God, which is a way of storing treasures in heaven.

Jesus implies that either money or concern for the kingdom of God can capture the heart. The one leads to our ruin. The other leads to our spiritual health.

One time Jesus was observing how people were giving to the temple treasury. The rich gave out of their extra wealth, probably without suffering at all. Suddenly a poor widow came by. Jesus spoke as if her two mites (a fraction of a cent) were all the money she had. Yet in the goodness of her heart she gave them to the Lord's work.

The Savior praised her highly. She had, he said, given more than all the rich. She had offered her last resources simply because she wanted to give what she had to the Lord. (See Mark 12:41-44.)

Concerning wealth, Jesus taught—and the early Church practiced—*generous sharing*. Christ's concern was not in making shrewd investments, which will pay handsome dividends, but in giving generously to those in need.

When the rich young ruler asked Jesus how to find eternal life, Jesus pointed him to the commandments of God. This was nothing new—the rich man had obeyed the commandments since he was a boy.

Jesus quickly put his finger on a cold spot in the young man's heart. He was chained to his wealth! Jesus told him to get rid of his attachment to wealth, which was destroying his spiritual life.

Conquer this sin by giving your wealth to the poor, Jesus seems to be saying. That will transfer your treasure to heaven! Then come and follow me (Luke 18:18-30).

When the rich ruler heard that saying, his face fell. He went away very sad. As he left, Jesus looked at him and said to him, "How hard it is for those who have riches to enter the kingdom of God!"

Yet Jesus did suggest that even a rich man could be saved by God. And 1 Timothy 6:17-19 gives special instruction to the rich. This passage repeats Christ's basic instructions. It assumes some Christians will be rich—but warns them against pride, commands generous sharing, and promises they will thus lay up treasures in heaven.

The apostles and the early Christians believed that *wealth is for sharing*. Luke tells us in Acts 2:44 and 4:32 that the early Christians were so filled with divine love through the spirit of God that they had all things "in common."

What did Luke mean to tell us? Was he proposing a new economic system, some sort of communal plan? Was the church to become a vast corporation? Luke probably did not mean a new economic system, but a new spirit of generosity.

Acts 4:32 suggests that there was a remarkable unity of love in the church, a spirit of mutual concern. The several members still had possessions. But no one acted as though they were just for personal needs.

In other words, you have a ten-dollar need of some sort. So I reach into my wallet and give you the ten dollars. They are not really mine. Love compels me to share with you of what I own to help you through your need.

This was the spirit of the early church—each one lived for the good of the other. Everyone looked out for their neighbor's welfare (1 Cor. 10:24).

Luke's comments may not apply directly to the economic systems of our world. But they do challenge us to ask whether we can support policies that allow our world's rich to get richer while millions of poor people get poorer. What a beautiful planet we would have if the early church's attitude spread worldwide!

Putting Christ First

Christians are tempted to put family concerns first in their lives. Jesus taught his followers that if they wanted to be his disciples, they would have to put God first in their lives. Father, mother, wife, children, brothers, and sisters, and one's own self would need to come second (Luke 14:26; Matt. 10:37).

The Anabaptists tried to live by this sharp demand. Some of them were gone from home for long periods of time, preaching the Word and seeking to extend the cause of Christ. Sure enough, the critics were ready to condemn such unusual obedience as "not looking after one's family properly." Actually, the congregation tried to see that all the needs of one's family were met in such cases.

Now, of course, unprecedented pressures threaten the health of our families. Jesus' command to put God first remains applicable. But in a time when the way of the world is to put family behind so many other pleasures and demands, putting family first may sometimes be a way of putting God first.

FOUR

Living Closer to Christ's Teachings

The Christian faith is based upon a number of basic principles. One of these is faithfulness to God in daily living. This is sometimes called *discipleship*.

CHRIST'S FAITHFUL DISCIPLESHIP

The Son of God became human so Jesus might not only tell us of God and God's will, but also show us how God wants us to live. God truly became a man and was as human as we are. Jesus was tempted in all points as we are, yet he never sinned (Hebrews 4:15).

Jesus was faithful to God. He did not yield to Satan's temptations. Satan had some suggestions about easy ways to set up the kingdom of God. But Jesus was faithful to God.

Jesus was human *and* completely filled with God's presence. Some New Testament writers even call Jesus God (John 1:1). As the ancient confession puts it, "Very God of very God." This paradox—a truth seemingly contrary to human reason—lies at the heart of Christian faith.

For Jesus, discipleship also meant suffering. Israel could not grasp the nature and work of the coming Savior, the Messiah (in Greek, the Christ). Many prophecies refer to this coming one as a King. He would be of the family of David, and would occupy the throne of David. He would reign and prosper. He would deliver his people. He would be a conquering hero like King David had once been.

Yet the prophecies about the suffering servant, such as Isaiah 53, suggested that the suffering servant would not be attractive. Rather, he would be despised and rejected. He would grieve, be familiar with suffering.

Isaiah portrays Christ's suffering as vicarious, as substitutionary—suffering for us. He would bear our sorrows and his side would be pierced with a sword. Through his punishment we would enjoy *peace*—that is, total well-being and full acceptance by God.

Through Jesus' wounds we would receive healing and spiritual health. No longer would we need to live in hopeless guilt and fear of facing the future. The high point of the entire suffering servant section in Isaiah 53:6 is this:

All we like sheep have gone astray;
    we have turned every one to his own way;
and the Lord has laid on him
    the iniquity of us all.

The New Testament writers report in great clarity the life and teaching, the suffering and death, the resurrection and enthronement of Jesus the Messiah (Christ).

Before Jesus' death and resurrection, the disciples seemed uneasy about the nature of the kingdom Christ was establishing.

Just two generations before Christ, the hated Romans had crushed the Jewish Maccabean kingdom. The disciples were hoping Jesus would set it up again.

Thousands of Jews would have joined the cause had Jesus announced a military drive to push the Romans into the sea. The Jewish party called the Zealots waited eagerly for that great day to come.

DISCIPLESHIP IS BASED ON LOVE

All through his ministry, Jesus tried to tell his disciples that he was not going to take the sword to accomplish his mission. Rather, those who use the sword will surely perish by the sword (Matt. 26:52).

Time after time Jesus sought to make clear that he would fulfill God's commission, not by crushing enemies with physical might, but by suffering love. The shadow of the cross fell across the face of Jesus all through his ministry.

The Gospel of John tells us this clearly. "Destroy this temple," Jesus said of his earthly body, "and in three days I will raise it up" (John 2:19). Jesus told his hearers that the "bread" they really needed was his flesh, which he would give for the life of the world. John 7:33 is even clearer: "I shall be with you a little longer, and then I go to him who sent me."

Jesus tried hard to give his disciples an awareness of being under divine care. He said he was the Good Shepherd. The Good Shepherd lays down his life for the sheep (John 10:11,15,17-18).

When Mary anointed him with the expensive perfume, he said she had anointed him for the day of his burial (John 12:7). To the alarmed Greeks who feared for his life, Jesus laid down the eternal law of life. "Unless a grain of wheat falls to the earth and dies, it remains alone; but if it dies, it bears much fruit" (John 12:24).

Jesus could, therefore, challenge Peter, who tried to defend him: "Shall I not drink the cup which the Father has given me?" (John 18:11).

DISCIPLESHIP AS CROSS-BEARING

Jesus came to suffer the pain of the cross. Mark reports three separate occasions when Jesus openly tried to tell the disciples that he was destined to die and to rise again (Mark 8:31; 9:31; 10:32-34). Indeed, the death of our Lord was the sacrifice which, like a ransom, would set us free from the bondage of that sin which has kidnapped us (Matt. 20:28; Mark 10:45).

After his resurrection, Christ could rebuke his disciples for overlooking the suffering servant prophecies in the Old Testament. He accused them of being "slow of heart" to believe all that the prophets had written. He asked, "Was it not necessary that the Christ should suffer these things and enter into his glory?" (Luke 24:26).

The disciples had not applied the passages about the suffering servant to the Messiah at all. They could not grasp the idea that it was the will of God for the Messiah to accomplish his mission by dying.

The disciples simply could not grasp the possibility that Jesus would overcome by dying, that in defeat Jesus would win. As happens to us as well, because Jesus' life and teachings go against the grain of all our beliefs, they did not truly listen to Jesus. They did not truly hear when Jesus said that the poor are blessed, the meek will inherit the earth, the last will be first, we live by dying.

But this is Jesus' way, and what a fresh way it is in a world which is sick of those who win by crushing and hurting others. Jesus says that if we give up our old ways, if we die to our old selves, the new way he showed us and made possible by dying for us can be our way. We can then share that new way with the entire world.

During the forty days after his resurrection, Jesus continued to explain the Scriptures and how he fulfilled prophesies concerning the Messiah (Acts 1:3). He helped them understand that pictures of the suffering servant were better guides to who he was than pictures of conquering heroes like King David.

Just before his ascension, he told the disciples to wait in Jerusalem until they received the fullness of Holy Spirit baptism. So they waited, and in ten days the prophecy in Joel 2 was fulfilled during the Feast of Pentecost (fifty days). So we speak of the coming of the Holy Spirit as Pentecost.

A NEW VISION

On that great day of Pentecost, the Holy Spirit came upon the disciples (Acts 2). Now the Christians understood that one must die to the old to gain the new. Now they fixed their concern on the good news of the gospel.

This good news is that anyone who turns from sin and makes the surrender of faith will find that forgiveness and spiritual healing in Christ which is salvation.

Now the early Christians clearly saw the good plan of God. Christ had to suffer for our redemption before being exalted to the right hand of God. The New Testament writers regularly used the word the Romans used for their emperor to describe Christ. He is our "Emperor," our reigning Lord. Our vision now is to share his lordship over sin and death with others.

CHRIST IS OUR EXAMPLE

The suffering of Jesus, followed by his defeat becoming victory in God's hands, is also God's plan for Christians. We too are called upon to suffer here and now. We are not promised an easy life when we become disciples.

Jesus said that the disciple is not above a master. If the head of the church had to bear reproach and suffering, the disciples can expect no less (see Matt. 10:21-25).

The church of the Middle Ages had lost sight of the suffering servant passages in the New Testament. The church, therefore, did not see itself as a suffering body. Thus, it made the same mistake as did those who held to the doctrine of a royal Messiah.

In contrast, the Anabaptists of the Reformation era emphasized the suffering motif of Scripture. In their teaching of suffering with their Lord, they spoke of him as the "bitter Christ."

TAKING UP OUR CROSSES

Jesus said that as Christ's disciples we must forget ourselves, take up our crosses, and follow Christ in daily life (Luke 9:23). The Anabaptist Hans Denck understood this teaching of a suffering church. Denck said, "No man can truly know Christ unless he follows him in life."

This teaching of cross-bearing is central in Anabaptist-Mennonite doctrine. All Anabaptist literature emphasized it. In 1554 Menno Simons wrote a major book on *The Cross of the Saints*.

Jesus warned us that if the world hates us, we know that it first hated him (John 15:18). When Paul and Barnabas were instructing converts in the Roman world, they warned them of suffering.

We must through much tribulation enter into the kingdom of God (Acts 14:22). The apostle Peter asks who will harm us if we do only good? (1 Peter 3:13). Many, unfortunately. Peter enlarges on the theme in 4:12-16. "Do not be surprised," he wrote, "at the fiery ordeal which comes upon you . . ., but rejoice in so far as you share Christ's sufferings"

The first Anabaptist leader, Conrad Grebel, predicted that he and his colleagues would suffer persecution because of their call for the separation of church and state. And suffer they did.

ANABAPTISTS SUFFER AND WITNESS

Perhaps the most influential book in Mennonite history is Tieleman J. van Braght's famous *Bloody Theater* or *Martyrs Mirror* (1660). This huge book of more than 1,100 pages is an enlargement of several earlier martyr books. It has been reprinted in Dutch, in German, and in English.

In this book we can read of the savage torture and cruel and inhuman deaths of countless Anabaptist-Mennonite martyrs. Some five thousand sixteenth-century Anabaptists died for their faith, about half in the Netherlands and Belgium, and an equal number in Switzerland, South Germany, and Austria.

A Hutterite summarizes this period of suffering. After the Hutterite *Chronicle* had reported the deaths of well over 2,000 martyrs, the editor wrote:

Many were dealt with in wonderful ways . . . with great craftiness and roguery; also with many sweet and smooth words, by monks and priests, by doctors of theology, with much false teaching and testimony, with many threats and menaces. . . .

As some of them lay in grievous imprisonment they sang hymns of praise to God, as those who are in great joy. Some did likewise as they were being led out to death . . . as those going to meet the bridegroom at a wedding they sang out joyfully with uplifted voice that rang out loudly. . . .

From the shedding of this innocent blood arose

Christians everywhere. . . . Many were moved thereby to serious thought, and to order their lives. . . . Finally the executions were carried out at night, as in the county of Tirol . . . in secret and at night so that not many people would see, hear, or know of them. . . .

In some places they filled the prisons and jails with them, as did the Count Palatine on the Rhine, supposing that they could dampen and extinguish the fire of God. But in prison they sang and were joyful. Nothing was of any avail. . . . They endured all sorts of torture and pain. Some had holes burned through their cheeks.

Everywhere much slander and evil was spoken of them, that they had goats-feet and ox-hoofs . . . that they had their wives in common . . . that they slew and ate their children.

But when our Lord Jesus Christ will come in flaming fire, with many thousands of angels, to hold the judgment on this great Day, everything will again come forth. . . .

But the holy martyrs of God who are now in every distress will enter upon and receive a beautiful crown, a glorious kingdom, a great joy, a heavenly rest, an eternal life. . . .[3]

This is an example of what obedience to Jesus' teachings meant to the Anabaptists. Today many Christians who take discipleship seriously are experiencing similar suffering. Christians who live where life is safe and comfortable, where it is easy to become careless and indifferent, need to dedicate themselves anew to follow Christ.

Often, of course, "taking our cross" does not mean literally dying. It simply means following Jesus' teachings and examples day by day, no matter where the path may lead.

Notes

1. From *The Foundation Series* story collection, used by permission of The Foundation Series Publishing Council, Nappanee, Indiana; Newton, Kansas; Scottdale, Pennsylvania.
2. Ibid.
3. Translated from the German *Geschichtbuch*, pp. 237-241.

For Further Reading and Study

Armour, Rollin Tely, *Anabaptist Baptism*. Herald Press, Scottdale, Pa., 1966

Bender, Harold S, *The Anabaptist Vision*. Herald Press, Scottdale, Pa., 1955

_____, *The Anabaptists and Religious Liberty*. Augsburg Fortress Press, Minneapolis, 1970

_____, Ed. *The Mennonite Encyclopedia*, Vols. I-IV. Herald Press, Scottdale, Pa., 1955-59

Driver, John, *Understanding the Atonement for the Mission of the Church*. Herald Press, Scottdale, Pa., 1986

Durnbaugh, Donald F., *The Believers' Church: The History and Character of Radical Protestantism*. Herald Press, Scottdale, Pa., 1985

Dyck, Cornelius J., Ed. *Introduction to Mennonite History*. Herald Press, Scottdale, Pa., 1981

Dyck, Cornelius J. and D. Martin, Eds. *The Mennonite Encyclopedia,* Vol. V. Herald Press, Scottdale, Pa., 1990

Friedmann, Robert, *The Theology of Anabaptism.* Herald Press, Scottdale, Pa., 1973

Hershberger, Guy F., *War, Peace, and Nonresistance.* Herald Press, Scottdale, Pa., 1969

Hostetler, John A., *Mennonite Life.* Herald Press, Scottdale, Pa., 1983

Jeschke, Marlin, *Believers Baptism for Children of the Church.* Herald Press, Scottdale, Pa., 1983
_____, *Discipling in the Church: Recovering a Ministry of the Gospel.* 3rd. ed., Herald Press, Scottdale, Pa., 1988

Kraybill, Donald B., *The Upside-Down Kingdom.* rev. ed., 1990

Kreider, Alan, *Journey Towards Holiness: A Way of Living for God's Nation.* Herald Press, Scottdale, Pa., 1987

Kreider, Eleanor, *Enter His Gates: Fitting Worship Together.* Herald Press, Scottdale, Pa., 1990

Mennonite Confession of Faith. Herald Press, Scottdale, Pa., 1963

Weaver, J. Denny, *Becoming Anabaptist.* Herald Press, Scottdale, Pa., 1987

Wenger, J. C., *Introduction to Theology.* Herald Press, Scottdale, Pa., 1976
_____, *Separated Unto God.* Reprinted by *Sword and Trumpet*, Harrisonburg, Va., 1990

The Author

Before his retirement, J. C. Wenger was a professor of historical theology at Associated Mennonite Biblical Seminaries, Elkhart, Indiana. He has made a lifelong study of Anabaptism and has published many articles and books in the field.

He studied at Eastern Mennonite and Goshen colleges (B.A.), at Westminster and Princeton Theological seminaries, and at the universities of Basel, Chicago, Michigan (M.A. in philosophy), and Zurich (Th.D.).

He taught at Eastern Mennonite and Union Biblical (India) seminaries. He served on the Committee on Bible Translation which prepared the *New International Bible*.

Wenger is a member of the Evangelical Theological Society. He has served on the editorial boards of the *Mennonite Quarterly Review, Studies in Anabaptist and Mennonite History*, and *The Mennonite Encyclopedia*, and on the executive council of the Institute of Mennonite Studies.

He has served the Mennonites (Mennonite Church) as a deacon, a minister, and bishop. He has been a member of their Historical Committee, Publication Board, Board of Education, district and general conference executive committees, and the Presidium of the Mennonite World Conference.

He married the former Ruth D. Detweiler, a registered nurse, in 1937. They are the parents of two sons and two daughters.

Blessed are they that have not seen,
and yet have believed.
–*John* 20:29

To my Joe,
who will always be missed more than I can say.

ONE

Traces of fog lingered along the East River despite the rapid warming of the August morning. Off-duty police officer Vivienne Armstrong paused at the fence bordering the Brooklyn Heights Promenade to gaze across the river at the majestic Manhattan skyline. Her city. Her home.

Slight pressure against her calf reminded her why she was there, and she smiled down at her K-9 partner. "Yes, Hank, I know. You want to run and burn off energy. What a good boy."

The soft brown eyes of the black-and-white border collie made it seem as though he understood every word, and given the extraordinary reputation of his breed, she imagined he might. She was wearing shorts and a sleeveless shirt for jogging, and her K-9 was also out of uniform. Put a regular collar and leash on him, and he behaved like any other dog. Show him

his tracking harness, and he was more than
eager to work instead of play. It was uncanny.

Vivienne adjusted the band of her sun visor
to lift her short dark hair off her forehead,
pivoted to check her surroundings and commanded, "Heel," as she started out. Hank kept
perfect pace at her side. "Good boy. You know
I love you, right?"

His tongue lolling, the canine met her gaze
with the equivalent of a doggy smile.

Under working conditions, she wouldn't
have distracted her dog with chatter, but their
time off was different. Besides, she reasoned,
Hank was family, her furry baby, particularly
since she was beginning to despair of ever
finding a good man and raising human children.

That was one of the drawbacks to exercising
on the Brooklyn Heights Promenade. It was almost always crowded with other people's children, mothers and nannies enjoying an outing
with their charges—darling little people who
had their whole lives ahead of them and the
wonders of the world yet to discover.

A piercing scream jarred her back to reality.
Hank barked, circling at the end of the leash.
Vivienne skidded to a halt and listened, look-
ing for the source.

"Jake! My baby! Where's my baby?" a woman screeched.

Other passersby froze, making it easy for Vivienne to pick out the frantic young woman darting from person to person. "He has blond hair. Bright green pants. Have you seen him? Please!"

There was no need for Vivienne to give Hank orders. The dog followed her rapid response perfectly.

"I'm a police officer," Vivienne told the hysterical woman. "Calm down and tell me what happened. What's your name?"

The fair-haired mother was gasping for breath, her eyes wide and filling with tears. "My little boy was right here. Next to me. I just… I just stopped to look at the boats and when I turned to pick him up and show him, he was gone!"

"Okay, Mrs…."

"Potter. Susanna Potter."

"Where were you when you last saw your son?"

She pointed with a shaky hand. "Over there. By the fence. Jake's always been a good boy. He's never wandered away like this before. I didn't dream…"

Vivienne could tell the mother was about to lose control again, so she led her to a bench

while she called in the report on her cell phone. "Sit here, Susanna."

"No! No, we have to go find Jake."

"I'm on the phone with the police," Vivienne explained, adding a description to her verbal report. "Jake Potter. Blond hair." She looked to the mother. "Is that right?"

Susanna nodded. "And bright green pants. There's a picture of a duck on his yellow T-shirt."

"Age?"

"Two—almost three. He's very precocious. Smart. Sweet. Wait! I have a picture on my phone." She was unable to hold her hands still so she handed the cell to Vivienne, then covered her face and began sobbing.

She repeated the description of the child's clothing. "Two years old, almost three. I'm with the missing child's mother at the promenade, close to Pierrepont Street. I'm sending you a photo from Mrs. Potter's cell phone."

She paused to listen, then said, "Copy. Hank is with me on scene. I'll see what we can do until backup arrives."

Seating herself next to the distraught mother, Vivienne gently touched her shoulder. "I'm a K-9 officer and my dog is trained for search and rescue. Do you have any item of your son's clothing that I can use for scent?"

"No. It was too warm for a jacket." Tears

streaked Susanna's pale cheeks and she was choking back sobs.

"Anything. A hat, a toy, anything Jake touched."

The woman blinked rapidly. "Yes! In my bag."

Vivienne watched as Susanna pulled out a well-loved, yellow, stuffed toy rabbit. "Perfect."

When she stood, so did the frantic mother. Vivienne blocked her with an outstretched arm. "No, please, ma'am. You need to wait here in case Jake comes back looking for you. Other police officers will be here in a few minutes, too." Vivienne wanted to know where to find Susanna when she needed her again. If she did. The sooner she and Hank got moving, the better their chances of finding the lost child.

Assuming he's merely lost, she mused, feeling her stomach knot. New York was a big city, and Jake was a tiny little boy. Without Hank's training, the chances of locating him were very slim. Even with the skilled K-9 there were no guarantees. Children were kidnapped all the time, many never seen again.

Except in this instance a rapid rescue was a possibility. She bent to present the stuffed rabbit and watched her K-9 sniff it, clearly ready to go to work.

In full professional mode, she straightened, loosened her hold on the dog's leash to give him leeway and commanded, "Seek."

Hank circled, returned to the place at the river fence that Susanna had indicated earlier, then sniffed the air before making up his mind and beginning to run.

The leash tightened. Vivienne followed as hope leaped, then sank. The dog was following air scent. Therefore, the missing child had not left footprints when he'd parted from his mother. Someone had lifted and carried him away. There was only one conclusion that made sense.

The little boy had been kidnapped!

FBI agent and profiler Caleb Black was in conversation with Sergeant Gavin Sutherland, head of the Brooklyn K-9 Unit, which had been formed just months ago, and the deputy police commissioner. They were inside a meeting room in the appellate courthouse in Brooklyn Heights to easily accommodate the commissioner, who'd had a press conference there earlier. The sergeant wrapped up what he knew about the department's ongoing efforts to locate a recently identified murder suspect, Randall Gage. A twenty-year-old investigation into the shooting deaths of the Mc-

Gregors, a married couple with two children, had been revived after a very similar double homicide. The MO in the current case involving another couple, the Emerys, was almost identical, down to the killer sparing the life of the victims' young daughter, Lucy, just as he had left Penelope McGregor unharmed many years before. It was going to be up to Caleb Black to compare clues, a clown mask and a stuffed monkey toy, and decide if the same murderer was truly back in action, or if they had a copycat on their hands.

Gavin stood and offered his hand to each man in turn, concluding their meeting. "Thank you for joining us, Commissioner. We appreciate your assistance, Agent Black."

"Anything I can do, Sergeant," Caleb replied, shaking hands with him. "Before I write up a formal profile, I'd like to speak with the survivor you mentioned. Penelope McGregor?" The McGregors had a son, too, ten years older than Penelope, but he hadn't been home during the murders; in fact, for a while Bradley McGregor had been considered a suspect. Fully cleared, he was now a detective with the K-9 unit. "I know it's been twenty years since her parents were murdered but sometimes the smallest detail will give me a lead."

"Fine. Penny's our front-desk clerk. We can

head over to the K-9 unit building now and you can also meet the team. I'm very proud of them."

"I've heard great things," Caleb said. "I hope they won't mind outside help on the case."

"We're all looking for the same result—justice for the McGregors and Emerys. So I think you'll find the K-9 unit accommodating. I take it that's not always the case?"

Caleb chuckled and raked his fingers through his short, dark blond hair. "Unfortunately, no, it isn't. I don't go out of my way to step on anybody's toes, but it can happen. Please keep that in mind as we work together."

"Noted." Gavin gestured toward the door of the conference room. "After you."

Caleb exited. He'd meant the compliment about this unit. It had been formed by bringing in K-9 officers from all around the city and seemed to be functioning cohesively despite its short history. That said a lot about its leadership.

As they were walking down the hallway, Caleb heard the sergeant's cell phone ping. Gavin paused to read the text, then hurried to Dispatch.

When Caleb caught up to him, he was being briefed. The news didn't sound good. An off-duty K-9 officer was reporting suspicions of

a child kidnapping. Before he had a chance to volunteer his services, Gavin drafted him.

"You can ride with me," the sergeant said. "We're very close to the promenade and hopefully we'll meet up with my tracker there. She and her K-9 were already on scene and have picked up the boy's trail."

"Got it." Much of Caleb's work was done in an office or on a computer, so a chance to work in the field was a welcome change. That, and he was looking forward to assisting a special unit like this one. Their success was his success.

Besides, he reasoned as he climbed into the passenger seat of a patrol car while the sergeant slid behind the wheel and prepared to drive, anything that helped find an innocent child was always his first priority.

Sobering, he fought against the memories of losing his own family. No matter how many days, months and years passed, the ache—the emptiness—remained. So did the weight of guilt. He should have done more, should have protected his wife and baby. But he hadn't been vigilant enough. He'd been so focused on doing his job he'd lost sight of the danger to his loved ones.

Caleb's jaw clenched. His beloved wife was gone and so was his only son. That couldn't

be changed. But he could do his best to protect other people's children. And he would. For the rest of his life. Regardless of personal cost.

Panting, Vivienne trailed her dog. Hank was straining so much that his collar was making him cough, but there was no time to go home for his tracking harness. Keeping him out of trouble during his reckless dash along the promenade was the best she could do.

A flash of bright green and yellow in the crowd caught her eye. Then it was gone. Could she have imagined seeing the colors? Any error was possible for human senses. Hank, on the other hand, was positive they were on the right track. Vivienne trusted the intelligent, dedicated K-9 beyond her own eyes. If he believed Jake was ahead, then he was. The only question was how far.

They dodged a woman pushing a double stroller with twins then barely missed an oblivious jogger wearing earbuds. "Excuse me. Pardon me," Vivienne shouted. "Police officer in pursuit!"

Up ahead, someone in a dark gray hoodie pivoted and glanced back at her. That was all the confirmation it took. A little blond boy wearing bright green pants and a yellow

T-shirt was crying and pushing at the tall, middle-aged woman carrying him off in her arms.

"Stop! Police," Vivienne shouted. She had to catch up. Once their quarry left the promenade it would be harder for Hank to track. Plus, the kidnapper might have a car waiting. Her K-9 partner was good, but no dog could follow a closed vehicle in Brooklyn traffic.

Sides heaving, laboring to breathe, Vivienne pressed on. Her legs ached. She had a stitch in her ribs. Adrenaline kept her going while her exhausted body screamed for her to stop. To give up.

"No way," she muttered, positive she was close enough to hear the wailing little boy in spite of the noisy chaos around her. Whoever the woman was, she was carrying the extra weight of the child. Surely a physically fit officer and her K-9 could overtake them in time.

Dear Lord, give me the strength to do this! she prayed silently.

Gathering herself, she shouted again. "Police officer. Stop! Let the boy go."

Did the abductor falter? It looked like it. "I said, freeze. Put down the child."

Over the cries of the boy, the shouts of passersby and Hank's barking, Vivienne thought she heard a siren. *Hurry, hurry, hurry*, she thought. *Block the street exit.*

Suddenly, the woman in the hoodie staggered. Almost fell. She regained her footing only to trip again. The strain of the foot pursuit was showing, and she had apparently realized she was not going to escape as long as she was weighed down by her victim.

Little Jake looked surprised when the kidnapper set him down none too gently. He plopped onto his bottom and raised a renewed cry.

Hank closed in. Vivienne was right behind him. She watched the hoodie disappear into the crowd as she approached Jake Potter in all his weepy, sweaty, red-faced glory. She quickly called 911 and identified herself, then relayed the description of the kidnapper. A BOLO would be sent out immediately.

Fighting to catch her breath, she pocketed her phone and bent over, hands resting on her knees, and grinned at the child. She'd never seen a lovelier sight.

"Hey, Jake, it's okay. You're safe now." Still panting, she reached for him. "I'm going to take you back to your mommy."

The child was too frightened to respond to her kindness and attempted to scramble away. Vivienne plunked down on the ground beside him, offered him his stuffed bunny to keep him close and used her cell phone to relay a

full description of the abductor and news of Hank's success. Then she lavished the K-9 with praise instead of paying undue attention to the child. In moments she was able to ease Jake into her lap. The border collie provided comic relief by trying to lick her face. And Jake's.

This was why she was a cop. This was why she'd put off marriage and starting a family of her own. This kind of triumph made all those personal sacrifices worthwhile even though they had cut her off from normal opportunities to date. Circumstances had even driven her to explore online dating apps, which was more than a little embarrassing.

A yammering crowd was gathering. People were aiming cell phones and taking photos of the aftermath as Vivienne embraced the toddler and rejoiced. Uniformed officers soon got between them and the throng, insisting they be given breathing room.

"Thanks, guys. One of you loan me a radio, and I'll report."

"That won't be necessary," a voice from behind the closest officer announced. "Dispatch relayed your calls. We have a good description of the perp."

She recognized her commanding officer, Sgt. Gavin Sutherland, greeted him with a

broad grin and got to her feet with the boy in her arms. "Hey, Sarge. Can you send one of the uniforms to go get Susanna Potter? A frantic blonde woman. Waiting on the promenade. Straight up that way. At least I hope she followed my orders because I promised this little man I'd reunite him with his mommy."

Sniffling, the child wrapped his chubby arms around her neck. Her heart swelled. She reached into her pocket, searching for a tissue as she gently patted the boy's back.

A tall man with a crew cut and wearing a dark suit and tie stepped forward to offer her his folded pocket square. Reluctant to accept anything from a stranger, particularly something silk and so elegant, Vivienne hesitated.

Gavin said, "This is Caleb Black, FBI."

The profiler. *What was he doing out here?* "Sarge mentioned you'd be coming to the station today." She noticed a woman pushing a stroller nearby and asked for a baby wipe, then concentrated on cleaning the boy's face. "If I'd been expecting to babysit this morning, I'd have come better prepared."

Caleb tucked the square back into his chest pocket. "No problem."

The rumble of his deep voice skittered along her nerves and nearly made her shiver despite the heat. His gaze was fascinating, and per-

haps a little too intense. There was something about the green of his expressive eyes that reminded her of parks and trees...during a summer storm. His military-cut, light hair was on the blond side of brown, making it seem tipped with gold.

He glanced at her briefly before beginning to focus past her into the crowd. Vivienne realized what he was doing and appreciated the effort even if it did increase her nervousness. The FBI profiler was assessing the gaggle of observers, one by one, looking for anything out of the ordinary. Looking for threats.

She shivered. He was right. There was a strong possibility that Jake's kidnapper wasn't working alone, particularly if the attempted abduction was part of a child-trafficking ring like the one the NYC K-9 Command Unit had taken down in Brighton Beach last year.

Pulling Jake closer, she cupped the back of his curly blond head with her free hand and assumed a guarded posture.

Caleb Black gave a barely perceptible nod, clearly approving. He had only spoken two words to her, yet she felt as if they were already operating in sync. It was uncanny. And welcome.

TWO

Caleb picked out the boy's frazzled mother the instant she came into view. She was running, arms spread wide, weeping openly and calling to her son.

"Jake! Jake, baby!"

The child's tears returned, and he began to strain to escape Vivienne's protective embrace. Not only was she grinning at the frantic mother, but she also had misty eyes. It was not Caleb's place to judge the K-9 officer, but it worried him to see that much emotion on display. The best law-enforcement agents kept their feelings to themselves. Like he did. He had to, in order to function.

After observing the beginnings of the touching reunion, Caleb turned away. There was only so much emotional tenderness he could stand, and he wasn't about to watch when he didn't have to.

Gavin Sutherland left him to join a uni-

formed K-9 team that included an imposing-looking German shepherd.

Patrol officers had corralled the still semihysterical mother and were taking down her story while she clung to her son. The crowd began to disperse. Since the black-and-white dog and its handler were free at the moment, Caleb decided to bestow praise where it was due.

"Good tracking job," he told Vivienne. "That was a close call."

She nodded, balling up the soiled wipe. "Yes, it was. I don't see a trash can."

"Give it to me. I'll dispose of it for you," Caleb remarked, holding out a hand. The grin she immediately shot him was a little surprising under the circumstances. When she gave voice to her thoughts, however, it made perfect sense.

"Speaking as a member of an FBI Behavioral Analysis Unit, would you say that offer shows a tendency for chivalry, or is it an expression of obsessive cleanliness? Did you ever play in the mud as a child?"

He had to laugh. "Yes, I did. Let's call it both."

"Good to know."

Despite her light-hearted attitude, Caleb could tell the stress of the pursuit was starting to affect her so he gestured toward a nearby

bench. "Sit a minute? I'd like to hear everything that happened this morning."

"I guess it won't hurt." He saw her eye her boss before joining him. "Sarge can find us if he wants to debrief me."

"It's hard to miss you with that black-and-bright-white dog in tow. Is he a border collie?"

"Yes." She removed her sun visor, then raked her fingers through her long bangs and tucked the ends behind her ear. "Hank is search-and-rescue trained. In this case I was able to put him on the trail immediately so tracking was easier, even after the woman picked the boy up."

"You're positive the kidnapper was a woman?"

"Positive. I saw her face," Vivienne said.

"What tipped you off to the crime?"

With a nod toward the child and his mother, Vivienne explained. "Screaming. Mrs. Potter was yelling that her son was missing. I know kids wander away all the time and that's what I expected when I put Hank on the trail." She shivered despite the heat while her K-9 sat obediently at her feet.

"As soon as the medics are through checking the boy you should let them look you over, too. The intense physical and mental stress of what you just went through—"

"I'm fine. Worn out, but fine."

He nodded. "Good thing you and Hank were right there," he said, loosening his tie. "Gotta love August in New York."

"Where are you from? DC?"

"Not presently. We have a field office in the federal building in Manhattan and a resident agency—a satellite office—right here in Brooklyn. Why?"

"I just wondered." She eyed him up and down. "You look more like a CEO or a politician than an FBI agent."

"Maybe I'm in disguise," he said as he slipped his suit coat back on, added reflective sunglasses and squared his shoulders.

That comment brought a light laugh that pleased him. He didn't have a reputation for carrying on humorous conversations, but this K-9 cop seemed to bring it out in him.

"Now you look like Secret Service," Vivienne teased.

"Thanks. That's the image I was going for." It felt odd to be grinning at her after the serious incident. At least this time the outcome had been good. "What else can you tell me about the person in the hoodie?"

She squinted up at the tree providing shade, recalling all she could. "She turned around for only a split second, so I didn't have a long look,

but enough. Middle-aged. Tall and thin but not agile. She ran out of steam pretty quickly once we started chasing her. She wore shorts and I think she had varicose veins."

"Excellent. Hair color? Complexion?"

"Ruddy, although her face may have been flushed from exertion. I couldn't really see her hair under the hood. If it had been very dark or very light the contrast might have shown up. And I think there was an orange tattoo of a flower on her ankle. She was wearing flip-flops. They certainly hampered her running. That she didn't cover up an identifying detail and wore flip-flops makes me think the kidnapping was impulsive instead of the boy being a premeditated target."

"Either that or she couldn't afford better shoes. Besides, it is summer." He stared at her for a moment. "You told all that to Dispatch?"

"Of course. I may not be in uniform like Belle Montera over there with Justice, the German shepherd, but I assure you I didn't forget my training."

Caleb raised both hands, palms facing her. "Whoa. I wasn't being critical. Just wanted to be sure everything got done. I know you're exhausted and as soon as the rush of adrenaline wears off you'll be a zombie."

"Never," Vivienne snapped. "What you see now is what you always get."

Caleb muted a smile. This was a pretty, athletic, witty woman, and if his life hadn't been ruined by his past he might even have been interested in getting to know her better. That was not going to happen, of course. He'd learned his lesson the hard way. The most painful way possible. He'd been a devoted husband and father. Once. He wasn't about to risk that kind of pain again.

Without thinking, he used his thumb to touch the wedding band he still wore. Professional counselors and friends had urged him to take it off, but he wasn't ready. Perhaps he never would be.

Noting the K-9 officer's glance toward his left hand, he hoped she wouldn't ask about his marital status. An adequate explanation was still painful, yet few strangers were sensitive enough to keep from posing hurtful, personal questions once he revealed that he'd been widowed.

Caleb clenched his jaw. Might as well get it over with. He displayed his hand, fingers splayed. "Widower" was all he said.

Instead of having to fend off an inquisition he was relieved when Vivienne merely said, "Sorry," and turned away.

* * *

The last thing Vivienne wanted to do was admit the FBI agent was right about her physical stress. Unfortunately, as the minutes passed, her body agreed with him. The bottles of water the EMTs had given her and Hank had helped quench her thirst but hadn't done much to restore energy levels. This excessive fatigue wasn't unexpected, it was merely the aftereffect of intense physical exercise coupled with razor's-edge concentration.

Frustrated, she continued to picture the kidnapper's face, wondering if she'd be able to set aside preconceived notions well enough to work with a sketch artist. Maybe. Probably. The key would be visualizing the event, then stopping time in her mind to study the face in detail. That was difficult because the brain tended to fill in unknowns on its own.

"Ready to go?" Gavin Sutherland asked as he approached.

Vivienne wasn't sure whether he was speaking to her or to the FBI agent. "I walked over from my apartment, Sarge," she said. "I'll be fine getting home on my own." A stifled yawn punctuated the end of her sentence.

"Nonsense. You and Hank can hitch a ride with me. I'll take Caleb back to his car, anyway, which is parked near the courthouse, so